BEYOND ETERNITY

Beyond Eternity

An anthology of poems

by

EDWARD BONNER

Canonsburg
Karate

And

Self-Defense
Books

BEYOND ETERNITY

An anthology of poems

By Edward Bonner

Copyright © by Edward Bonner

For any information, please address to

Edward Bonner

edkarate@yahoo.com

Printed in the United States of America

Each Arrow Destined

I welcome you into the depths where bodies melt

through internal thoughts.

Scream to speak in this hidden bog of reality and reason.

Thanks to Unsplashed images and Pexels.

Contents

Preface

In presenting a few of the following adventures to
the public, factual and fictional stories are included
with my poetry writings from selected "quote-
prompts" to explain the internal meaning of life.

It is said that the truth is often more surprising than fiction;
and those in pursuit of this unique venture will not be
disappointed in these pages full of countless wonders.

To understand the "Way" is to look around you.
Relationship with life is a continuation
through acceptance in change.

The Oil Field

It wasn't just life; this was our world.
Rise and shine.
Breakfast is at seven in the morning.
"Cold cereal and then a dash out the door"

Four of my friends and I would run to the local
baseball field and play America's past time.
"Baseball'
Nicky; Matt; Luke and Bobbie were the players.
Nicky was my best friend. We were like a tag-team.
Matt and Luke were brothers.
They would always get on each other, especially
if one made an error in the game.
Bobby was a little older.
He was a pain in the butt.
Everything was his way.
"You know the kind"

Racing up Nansen Street, felt like running to
the top of mountain, only with potholes.
Trees protruded from each side of the road
consumed light making shadows come to life.

Reaching the top, we made a sharp
right onto Hazelwood Avenue.
Hazelwood Avenue was constructed
with "Belgium cut" stone blocks.

In the rain, the blocks were slippery as ice.
You would never ride a bike.
It would be wipe out city.
And the cars would creep five miles per hour down the hill.
Otherwise they would end up into someone's living room.

About a quarter of a mile walk and we
were standing at the backstop.
Now this baseball field was unique in its own way.
The locals called the field, the "Oil Field".
The proper name was the "Gladstone" field.
Which was the high school and grade school
located about a quarter of a mile away.

This field was sprayed monthly with oil.
Yes oil!
This prevented dust, mud, grass and bugs.
"Who would believe this today"?

The Oil Field was hard and fast.
You could smell the field a block away.
You definitely didn't want to slide.
But at all costs,
to win the game we did everything
and anything.
Slide, jump and roll.
Covered with a black type tar,
our clothes would be stained as our bodies would be in pain.
We were never allowed in the house with our shoes
on. That's when you would get a tongue lashing.

Now how the heck do you play a baseball
game with only five players?
The best way is.
One player between shortstop and third base,
the second player at left center outfield,
last the pitcher, first baseman and a catcher.
With a lefty batter, we would switch the outfield
player to right-center and short to second.

If a right-hand batter hits the ball to between second
base and first base he's automatically out.
With a left-hand batter, it will be the opposite. Hit
between second and third you were out.

Morning until dusk,
we played baseball all summer.
The girls would watch,
never allowed on the field.
Fear of staining their clothes and white tennis shoes.

There may be a few fights about certain plays on the field.
We'd be rolling around and look like
we're ready to be feathered.
Funny no one got hurt.

"Man, here comes the older kids"
"Them damn bullies"
They would kick us off the field so they could play.
One day they got out of hand.
Picking on us kids so freaking bad,

they started throwing equipment all over the field.
Gloves, bats and baseballs launched all over the place.

One kid, his name was Mick.
He looked like a sumo wrestler.
"A big fat dough boy"
Mick threw us around like rag dolls.
Swearing and calling us names.

We ran
and ran,
Empty handed and all.
Our equipment was left at the field.

When we reached home,
Nicky told his brother "Johnny" what
happened at the Oil field.
Johnny hopped on his minibike and sped up Nansen Street.

By the time we reach the field.
Johnny was powerlifting Mick over his head.
Johnny threw Mick on the hill side.
A hundred yards away, we heard a thud.
That was the last time these kids picked on us.

In the evening we would watch men
play softball on the Oil Field.
These players crushed the ball.
If they hit a ball in the outfield, you would lose sight of it.
Within seconds, the catch was made.

This was amazing.
Each player had grace, speed and power.

Spectators would be sitting on the
sidewalk cheering the players.
What a great evening.

Legend of the Razorback

One Saturday morning,
my cousin Lynda and I decided on a trip.
A trip to see Big Boy.
A vicious legend of a large ferocious boar.

Big Boy lived on a farm above the Oil field.
Deep into the woods in an area of no man's land.

Climbing to the top of the plateau,
our trek through the hills of oak, sycamore
and walnut trees was exciting.
Each step was fondly new in this unguided quest.

Crossing our favorite pond of lizards, frogs and turtles,
there was a "board like balance beam"
used to walk across the water.
One slip and you were knee high with mud soaked pants.

Now a tough crawl under the multi floral rose,
where the briars stuck to every part of your body.

Finally we arrived at the farm.
All of a sudden,
we hear barking coming toward us.
Then the sight.
Two Dobermans chomping, biting and spitting.
Charging at a speed so fast,

it was a blur
passing through the wind.

Frozen in our tracks.
Inches from my feet.
Covered with saliva.
I hear a whistle and yell.
"Prince! Cesar!"
And the dogs retreat.
One second longer
and my legs were going end up as dog bones.

Greeted by a man, his named was Johnson.
Polite and friendly, he introduced himself as the owner.
Lynda and I asked if we could tour the farm.
Rumors of a large boar pig, named Big Boy.
We would love to see.
"Sure he said."

His children came running.
Smiles from ear to ear,
Sam and Alicia were their names.
Inviting us to their farm,
we all chased the chickens and ducks.

An hour or so, they invited us for lunch.
Favorite kid's meal,
cheese sandwich.
"What more can you ask for!"

After lunch, our reason comes to mind.
Big Boy!
"Where is this monster?"
We beg.

"Come on we'll show you."
Sam blurted out.
We sprinted to the pen.
Oh my God.
The thoughts in our head.
In no time we arrived.

There was squared off wooden pen.
I hear the sound of snorting and slopping.
We jump to the top of the fence.
What we see is a monster.
A gigantic pig!
A Volkswagen Bug on four legs.
Hairs standing on end, it's Big Boy!

Alicia blurts out, "let's ride!"
Lynda and I shout, "what!"
"Come on. Don't be afraid."
With enough nerve we jump on Big Boy.

A baby of an animal we rode him up
and down through the mud.
After the fun and games, it was time to leave.
What a tremendous day.
Now we can go home and tell the true story of Big Boy.

Electric Street

Some mornings,
I would find myself walking
on a crumbling
asphalt road,
to a secluded creek,
hidden between homes and woodlands.

This road had an unusual name.
"Electric Street."
Electric Street held secrets only the locals were aware of.

The entrance to Electric Street sported a sign.
Dead End Street.
What's the first thought on your mind?
Dead End.
Where does this street lead to?

There's an eerie feeling when you make a wrong
turn and find yourself on a dead end street.
"No turning back".
"A disruption of flow to the mind",
"No exit".

At the end of Electric Street
sat a lonely old stripped stolen car.
Rusted beyond repairs, this automobile was an
exquisite home for mice, chipmunks and spiders.

Beyond this stolen car opened up into
a boy's outdoor amphitheater.

A small path lead through a green wooded canopy hovering
with wild grapevines, sumac and small plant shoots.

This oasis pillowed into a forest like atmosphere
flowing with beechnut, walnut and oak trees.

"Launching a new existence to exploration,
 this kid was ready to take on nature's hidden mysteries."

A small creek ran north to south.
Words came into mind like snakes, lizards and crayfish.
Words like rabbits, birds and chipmunks.
Words like muddy, wet and fun.

Catching lizards and crayfish you had to be quick and
 not too scared of sticking your hands under rocks.
Wearing a good pair of sneakers with decent tread was a plus.

Turning over each rock you had to be
 quick with your hands and feet.
Lizards were slippery slimy fast.
The crayfish sported a painful pinch,
 making the catch challenging.
The sight of a crayfish you must be smart.
Sneak behind his bug eye vision.
Slowly move your hand close enough for a quick catch.
Snatch that crustacean behind his claws, like

grabbing a person under their armpits.
The power is in the grasp, it must be strong and
yet soft not to crush the crayfish shell.
Once you catch a lizard or crayfish, they're
placed in a coffee-can admire.

As for snakes, capturing was a thrilling experience.
Sly as a cat, hid like a rat.
Fast and slithering just like that!

Garter, black or rat snakes were the most common in the area.
These snakes were always around creeks searching
for food, like minnows, tadpoles and bugs.

During the heat of the day was the best time to catch snakes.
They would creep out from under logs, rocks,
or animal burrows and bask in the sun.

You must be quiet when walking.
Each step was slow, scanning the area.
Be careful not to step on a garter snake. It may
injure them, but it will almost certainly frighten
them enough to run away or bite you.

A great tool to use catching these sly reptiles is a forked stick.
Pin the snake down and let him thrash
around until exhausted.

Some kids like to pick the snake up by the tail.
I was always afraid to get bitten.

I would grab or pinch at the cheek, behind their mouth.
That was a suffice capture.

Sometimes I would bring them home as pets.
My grandmother wasn't too thrilled.
One day I had eight in a plastic aquarium.
Slipping down the steps,
I dropped the aquarium on the cellar floor.
All the snakes escaped.
I recovered five.
I never said anything about the other three.

Shadows begin to form.
Everything turns a grayish blue.
Finally it was time to head home.
Covered with mud, wet and stinking.
What a great day.

Thunder Under the Sky

Along the sheltered wood line,
oak trees speak within the soft breeze.
A white glow from the moon
reflects the early morning mist
rising from the warm earth.

The walk is a distance to the top.
The summit ascends with secrets held
in virtuous personalities.
A fresh spring smell is the beginning of life.

Entering the woodland,
a few dead dry cracking leaves lie underfoot.
Slow and easy,
careful not to fracture a limb.
I must be quiet not to wake the king of the mountain.

Sly like a fox;
this audacious tack is quite sharp.
Settling in;
I sat "back to tree" in hopes to raise "thunder" under the sky.

The morning sun invites the transformation
from dark to light.
Slowly life awakens...

To manage by trick.
A spell to conjure;

only with a gentle tease,
I would call in the soft breeze.

Yelp, purr, cluck, cackle.
Sounds like a comedy club.
Only, this is the mating call from a brood hen.

The king responds with a cosmic thundering gobble;
heard with intensity and magnitude his
response shatters the mountain side.

It is time to respond with a soft cluck,
making this beast ignite his vibes to mate.

Twenty minutes go bye.
Hot, inflamed, squirrelly,
he flies to the ground.

I cluck and purr.
It's quiet.
Minutes go bye, I cluck and yelp.
Suddenly a thunderous gobble
responds.

Closer!
He is approaching with power.
The mountain goes quiet.
I must have patience not to move.
His vision is like an eagle.
His hearing is like a deer.

I must stay calm.
Breathe softy.
Scan the area slowly without moving my head.

My body is fully camouflaged from head to toe.
Only my eyes are exposed;
watching the terrain for the slightest flicker.

Slowly scanning left to right up and down,
quiet is more than quiet.
Total concentration is beyond the depths of the abyss.

Finally sixty yards away is a dark movement behind a log.
I make one soft cluck.
Hell breaks out!
His sound is strong and mighty.
Proud and powerful he opens to show his size and beauty.

The gobbler begins to parade around in full strut,
presenting himself as the king of the mountain.

Pure,
powerful gobbles,
he is nearing the zone.
Where is his mate?
Is she hiding?
Closer he comes and spots the decoy hen.
He lets out a commanding request.
It shakes the hair on my neck.

He is in the zone!
Slowly I aim my shotgun at this magnificent bird.
The bead trained on his wattle.
Slowly I remove the safety.
My finger cradles the trigger.
I squeeze.

Exploding power recoils against my shoulder.
Pellets sent flying a light sulfuric smell permeates the air.

The end result;
the most memorable day of the year.

Little league baseball games,
baseball cards and the Pittsburgh Pirates.
What a combination.
Add all three and I'm going to be in the majors.

Every day running, hitting and throwing a baseball.
Baseball! Baseball!
A catcher!
I was going to be a catcher'
A professional baseball catcher.

Wednesday, July 07, 1971
8:05 p.m. game time.
The Pirates play the "Big Red Machine" Cincinnati Reds.
My grandfather,
"who I called dad"
was taking me to the game.

What a thrill.
The big freaking "Red Machine".
The Pirates and the Reds had a rival going for years.
It wasn't hate, it was to win.

Our best:
Roberto Clemente, Steve Blass, "chicken
hill Will" Willy Stargell,
Bill Mazeroski!!!!

Manny Sanguill'en, Al Oliver and more.
The best baseball can find.
All Stars galore.

Against their best:
Johnny Bench. George Foster, Tony Perez
and the guy you love to hate Pete Rose.

In fact,
all the players
played for the team,
played for the fans,
played to win.

Arriving at Three Rivers Stadium was an unbelievable sight.
Built only one year ago,
the magnificent complex viewed the
point of the famous three rivers.
The confluence of Allegheny and Monongahela
rivers form the Ohio river.

The stadium was packed with people.
Cheering, screaming and whistling'
The "wave" had not started in the United States.

Food vendors bellowing'
Peanuts!
Popcorn!
Crackerjacks!
Hotdogs and pop!
The free smells drove you crazy.

My grandfather bought me a hotdog with
relish, catch up and mustard.
A nice cold pop to quench my thirst'

The National Anthem played.
The crowd stood up faced the United States Flag.
The players stopped during warm-ups.
Hats off, right hand across their chest'
everyone was singing.
Watching, I noticed some people crying
in honor of our country.
The Vietnam War was coming to an end.
Four soldiers on the field saluted the flag.
One from the Army,
One from the Navy,
One from the Air Force
and one from the Marines.

First batter up was "Charlie Hustle" Pete Rose.
Pete sacrificed his body to win.
One day he ended a career of an opposition player.
First pitch; lined single up the middle.
Damn!
With a double play, the inning was over.

Bottom of the first'
Pirates turn to bat.
Single.
Out.
Single by Roberto Clemente'

A couple walks, two singles and the Pirates were up 5 runs.
What a great inning.

By the end of the game, the Pirates killed the Reds 9 to 3.
Good pitching and clutch hitting, that's all you need.

10 p.m. the game was over.
Heading home with my grandfather, I
fell fast asleep in the car.

The next day.
I was running, hitting and throwing a baseball.

I played baseball thru college and in the McKeesport
DAILY NEWS
SUMMER LEAGUE - (Pittsburgh).
I was a catcher just like Manny Sanguill'en.

Dinner Time for Spider

Every kid knows when you place an insect on
a spider web the inevitable happens.
The spider sits with infinite patience waiting
for the right time to snatch his prey.

A little jiggle, a little noise and the way he goes.
"Speed, attack, cover and return"
In the end it's dinner time.

Large overhanging branches extended like
hands ready to carry you away.
This tree can grow a majestic one hundred
and fifty feet high into the sky.
The circumference can reach eight feet. It would take
four to five kids holding hands to rap around this tree.
Green fruit would fall from the branches. The
fruit was as large as a baseball. You would never
see anyone park a car under the tree,
otherwise there would be dents covering
the hood, roof and trunk.
This tree known as a walnut tree was massive.

You could not eat the fruit right away.
Inside was like tar or black grease covering a nut. People
would gather peel and let sit for a time. Then crack and eat.

Alongside this walnut tree concealed an alley with no name.
This alley granted imagination and creativity, a dead
end utopia for all children in the neighborhood.
Every game you can think of was played on this street.

Bicycles jumping off wooden platforms
introducednew thrills for the young at hearted.
Sometimes we would compete to see how
airborne the bicyclists could go.
Every once in a while, there would be a wipe out.

No problem, get up and try it again.
The trick was to spring up at the end of wooden
jump, this would give you distance.

Baseball and football was always exciting.
During our baseball games each player
had to bat from the opposite side.
This made it difficult for the hitter.
The baseball usually traveled a short distance.
However the switch hitters killed the ball.

Tag football games were played on asphalt roads.
Tackle would be disastrous. There were too many
injuries. Sometimes there would be a few accidental
takedowns. The end would be result bloody
knees, elbows and a bump on the noggin.
Big boys crying all the way home.

Street hockey was pure unadulterated hockey.
All you needed was a ball, hockey stick and a goal.
Fast exhilarating competition drove a kid to win.
With a certain amount of time, we
alternated offensive and defense.
Of course checking was limited,
you would either end up against a brick
wall or down into the woods.

There were more games like kickball to wrestling.
We would be muddy beyond recognition.

Badminton, Frisbee and nights of hide and
seek throughout the neighborhood.

At the corner entrance to the alley sat a small one level house.
It was light blue in color, box shaped with a flat slanted roof.
The siding was similar to shingles on a roof, a
gritty type texture overlapping each other.
There was an older couple that lived in the home.
Volpi was their last name'
D'Angelo and Mabel two little Italians.
Babushka and all that floral color design.

While playing in the alley, you would see the
curtains open slowly and then close.
The curtains would open about two inches.
It was creepy, like a black cat
waiting for a mouse to devour.

This mysterious manner
didn't faze us kids
until one ghastly day.

One kid hit a baseball that traveled up to Volpi's house.
All of a sudden, a little lady dashed out the side-door,
snatched the ball and scurried back in the house. She
was fast like lighting striking a tree. Everyone was
dumbfounded upon seeing this little woman steal the ball.

What's next?
We'll go knock on the door and ask.

The Volpi's would not answer the door.
The widow curtains on the right side of the
door opened slowly then closed.
Not a word was said.
We just ran away.

This was the beginning to the end of great games,
but there was a day for revenge. Not!
Some bad boy grabbed a dead bird
and placed it in their mailbox.
Of course a neighbor spotted the kid in the
act and screamed at him to get it out.
End of story.

The Green Cadillac

There was warnings on the radio and television about a
dark green Cadillac with shaded windows, creeping up and
down the streets snatching children from neighborhoods.

In the stillness between light and dark, the city breathes
endlessly the hidden secrets playing out life's saga.

The tune "Gallows Pole" by Led Zeppelin would be
heard from a distance before the carnage erupts.
The exhaust smelled like death.
Blood and guts permeated the air.

Hangman! Hangman!
The gallows are open.
Bring your friends for the silver and gold.

Six months ago, there was a girl found murdered not more
than a mile from her home. Her name was Sara Green.

She had been strangled.

Sara was last seen getting off her school
bus on a Friday afternoon.
Her schoolbooks were found on the sidewalk.

A young man walking his dog Sunday morning
in Sutter's Park found Sara's body.

One leg stuck out from the side of a creek bed. Around her
neck was a green nylon rope tied to a stick and twisted.

A green Cadillac with tinted windows was spotted driving
around the park Saturday night. The music "Gallows Pole"
blasting from inside the car was heard a hundred yards away.

State and local police were doing everything
possible to find her killer.
A reward was offered but it has gone unclaimed.

The communities were frantic.
News all over the country about a young child murdered
and found at Sutter's Park. "Everyone should be
on a look out for a green Cadillac to
immediately call the authorities".

At this time,
all the scientific gadgetry in the world could
not find the killer and bring to justice.

A green Cadillac with tinted windows, smelled like death
and driving through the city was a mysterious demon.
The sound of "Gallows Pole" freak-out all the people.

A month later, it was a Wednesday night before Thanksgiving,
Carol Banner of Washington left her job at the mall.
It was a busy day at work. All the employees where
gearing up for the big "after Thanksgiving sales".
Carol was meeting friends at the movies.

The next morning, Carol's car was found off Stolt's
road in a ditch. She never made it to the movies.

Carol was in the trunk dead, strangled with
a green one inch thick nylon rope.
This time a note was posted on her forehead
saying, "Green is Beautiful".
Wednesday night there was a green
Cadillac seen parked at the mall.
Smelled like rotten eggs.

The next tragic event was December 23, Irene
Mary,a 17 year old left home to meet friends. Her
body was found along a dirt road beaten and
choked.
There was a green nylon rope with a
stick twisted around her neck.
A note pinned on her shirt that said,
"no silver, no gold".

The FBI, state police and local police where all on the case.
Fingerprints, blood tests, footprints, clothing andtire
marks were all collected for evidence.

The New Year comes fast.
Three days later on January 3, 1977.
Debra Ridge, 17, of North Wood Township,
disappeared while walking to the school bus stop.

Her body was discovered in Allegheny County, 8

days later, only a few miles from her home.

Debra had been strangled with a green nylon rope tide to
a cut off broom handle. And her hands were missing.
A note pinned to her forehead said,
"HANGMAN" In capital letters.

Not far from Debra's body, a hand was found.
The county coroner said the hand was not from Debra.

By the time of Debra's murder, residents
were more than frightened.
Parents walked their children to the bus stop,
many women stayed home at night. Weapons
of all types were being sold off the wall.

Months have gone by without any new evidence
with the murders or the Cadillac.
Until one day, two teenage boys were walking
across the old Glenwood Bridge after a day
of fishing in the Monongahela River.

The old rickety wood plank bridge
sounded like a disaster to happen.
You could see the river below between the wooden planks.

While three quarters across the bridge everything went
silent. The boys looked around; no cars were insight.
All the traffic had disappeared.

Minutes later, the wooden planks started vibrating.
From the structure of the bridge, you could
not see the far end. The arc was too high.

As the noise got louder, the teens didn't worry
 much about increased vibration.
"They assumed the cars were driving on the bridge".
 They started to hear music playing.
 It was the song Gallows Pole.
 They looked back to see a dark green
 Cadillac driving towards them.

The boys started running.
 The noise was getting closer,
 only a few yards behind them.

The Cadillac drove up beside the boys.
 The passenger window was down.
 The stench was unbearable.
 The boys turned to see who was in the car.
 The Cadillac was empty.
 No one was driving.

The boys stopped dead in their tracks.
 The Cadillac kept going.
 When the car reached the other end
 of the bridge it disappeared,
"only the smell of death in the air".

Grapes to Wine

Body covered in mud but with a tranquil smile.
Her arms held grapes to make Moscato wine.
The money she earns are pennies to a dime.

Morning until night,
"women harvested grapes from the healthiest vine".
Only the finest wines are prepared for the wealthiest lives.

Grapes to glass captivate a rich man's taste.
Cheers to the free world as arms embrace.

Late that night,
in a city booming of street-lights and bars.
A young man and his bride were walking,
gazing at the stars.

From around the corner
a toddler appeared.
With his arms reaching out
he had no fear.

Tagging along like a lost puppy dog.
This couple understands the final epilogue.

"A little disturbing and not knowing what to do".
"I turned to the boy and gave him my food".

Like a shadow from a cloud.
"Gone in seconds"
He takes the bag and runs off into the crowd.

Tired from a long day; the couple retreat to their hotel.
Walking back,
they peer around the corner to see a woman
crouched down with her baby eating their meal.

This woman from the fields looked up and smiled.

Ft. Lauderdale Harbor resort invites guests
to a breathtaking beachfront life-style.
A stunning saltwater pool and private beach are separated by
their own Lazy River, making this a grand vacation for plenty.

'Summer of 1969 the first time flying on an airplane".
"Fly me" Eastern Airlines Boeing 727.
Flight 1890 Pittsburgh to Ft. Lauderdale, 7:20 am.
Mother "Rosemary" and son "Edward"
heading south for paradise.
Unaware the devil's narcotic is to pursue a serene soul.
What can be said about an existing nightmare?
A significant past lives deep inside your brain.

A mother's flowing enjoyment gracefully sat
at the hotel's poolside watching "Eddie" play
with his newfound friend "Timmy".
Her naivety unveils innocence to the demonic strangers.
The stalker scatters grain steadily; everything
is visible, but deceitfulness is obscured.

The kids had a great time.
Every morning after breakfast they met up at the pool.
And they played; played until dusk.

On the fourth day, a couple walked up to Rosemary
and introduced themselves as Timmy's parents.

Diane and Steve.
This delightful pair raved about how well
the children were getting along.

Diane and Steve bought lunch for the kids, a couple
hotdogs, fries and soft drinks. Everyone had their own
blue canvas chaise lounge to relax and eat lunch.

As always, tanning lotion, darker than dark, Eddie's
skin turned him into a little Mexican.
Timmy had a fair complexion.
Covered like a mummy, except in the water, that's
when he turned into a floating red apple.

The next day, Rosemary and her son went
on a tour to the Everglades.
It was a 3 hour tour departing from Miami, capturing
the wild spirit of Florida's swamp ecosystem.
This was unique to see real prehistoric beasts floating
in the water. Wild alligators were everywhere, plus
tons of birds wading in their natural habitat.
Hot and muggy, the sights, the smells of dank moss,
fungus, cattails, water lily exciting and unusual.

The last stop was to see the Seminole
Indians. These were real Indians.
They had tables lined up selling their handmade jewelry.

One little Indian girl caught everyone's attention. She
was dressed in a leather deer skin garment, moccasin

shoes and a turquoise beaded necklace. She was a
precious soul and singing to her own tune while her
mother sold garments. They were inseparable.

After the day's tour, the ride back to the hotel was silent.
The humidity had taken its toll on all the visitors.

The next morning was the last day in
Florida. 5pm was departure.
Eddie was the first one in the pool.
Timmy and his family seemed too
appeared from out of the blue.
Diane and Steve started talking to Rosemary about
home and what time the flight was leaving Florida.

Rosemary stated around 5 pm they were
leaving the hotel at 2pm for the airport.
"We can drive you to the airport" quoted Diane.
"You can have lunch at our house, we only live
about 20 minutes from the airport".

Rosemary thought that was a wonderful idea.
The kids can stay longer in the pool.
But why were Diane and Steve staying at the hotel, when
they lived so close, "Maybe just to get away for a week".

After a great stay in Florida, it was time to depart.
Diane met Rosemary and her son in the lobby.
Packed everything in her car and they headed
to the house for a small lunch.

Pulling into the driveway, Steve and
Timmy were waiting at the door.
The kids ran to the Timmy's bedroom to play.

Playing they did.
Timmy had this plastic bowling pin. He loved to hit
people with. After a few thumps on Eddie's head.
Eddie kindly removed the pin and
slapped him around a few times.
He finally realized he wasn't going to win.

After the spanking, the kids went to eat lunch.
Eddie noticed something was wrong with his mother. She
had no smile. If she tried, you could tell it was fake.
She kept quiet.
Finally Rosemary said it was getting late and they had to go.
"Stay a little longer" Diane blurted out.
"We're 10 minutes away from the airport"
Eddie wanted to stay a little longer, but his mother said "we
have to go" with no smile and a tear flowing down her cheek.

They all went to the car and drove off to the airport. No one
was smiling except the kids in the back goofing around.
Palms trees were lining the streets. What was to be 10
minutes became a half hour and then an hour.
What Eddie could hear, was his mother
"TAKE US TO THE AIRPORT!
We will miss the flight".

Rosemary's hand started to shake. She
squeezed her son's hand hard.
Finally there was a sign, "5 miles to Ft. Lauderdale airport".

The family said we could come back anytime and
stay at their place. Timmy would love it.
Rosemary said we'll see, because it was hard
to get out of work and only being a single
mother the cost was expensive to fly.
They persisted and said they would pay for the flight.
They gave Rosemary their address so she can write to them.
They also gave Eddie a little dinosaur about 2
inches high. It was a yellowish color.

Finally at the airport departure side all the luggage
was dropped off. The baggage man tagged each
bag and gave the receipt to Rosemary.

Diane and Steve hugged them both.
And Timmy hugged Eddie.
At the gate you could see black lines by Rosemarie's eyes.
Tears were flowing and dark streaks running down her face.

On the airplane, Eddie gave the small dinosaur
to his mother to hold until he got home.
Touchdown in Pittsburgh was about 2 1/2 hours.

At home Eddie asked for his little yellow
dinosaur. His mother lost it.
"Let's mail them a letter, maybe they can send me one back"
That was the end.

Gratitude doesn't come naturally.
Whether it's bad that comes to you, or bad you did to

others. To bring the past up is to realize God guided
and protected them. His grace carried you through it.

Many years later, Edward found out what
happened to that letter and toy.
His mother threw them in the garbage.

They wanted to buy little Eddie from his
mother. They wouldn't take her to the airport.
She thought WE were going to die.

The Forest

When I'm alone in the forest,
I can hear the trees whisper to one another.
Ghostly it may feel but soothing to my soul.

Her breath breathes into me, making me real.
Cool clear touch, unforeseen to the earthly being.

Existence is the reason to believe in this gracious utopia.

Looking to the Northwest, Mount Katahdin could
be seen one hundred and twenty five miles away.
The largest mountain in the state of Maine is named
by the Penobscot Native American Indians.
"Meaning the Greatest Mountain", towers
fifty-two hundred feet in the sky.
Nothing could be compared to my young
age at this moment in time.
I was in awe.

A slick rattle snake charming a bushy black tail squirrel.
Within the snakes distance a strike occurs,
promising his delicious meal.
The rage of one the terror from the other, life goes on.

Wolves and dogs hunt together, traveling the
forest domain searching the weak.
Finally, a warm scent hits their nose,
slowly they commence to follow.

The alpha male creeps noiselessly along a low lying swamp
that's bellowing with black flies and mosquitoes.
Within yards a heady smell is detected underbrush.
Crouching low the alpha male pauses for a
moment, eyes dilated, tail quivering, every
muscle taunt to its utmost tension.

With a sudden leap, he pounces on his victim.
A lone male deer injured from a dual with
another male for dominance of their land.
Clamping on to the neck of this deer, the subordinate
canines completely dispatch the end result.

Within a few hundred yards, a clear powerful
river flows through the forest.

The Penobscot River is a 109-mile-long river in the state
of Maine. Including the river's West Branch and South
Branch increases the Penobscot's length to 264 miles,
making it the second-longest river system in Maine.

The landlocked salmon flourish on small
aquatic insects, larvae and nymphs from many
dwelling flies like mayfly and caddis fly.

Every once in a while, I would see a black bear rush out
of the woods, dive into the stream and pull out a large
salmon and feast on the side of the stream's bank.
"A meal to suffice the bear's appetite for many days".

Many of the black bears where hunted with dogs or baited in.
One outfitter, her name was Kathy.
Kathy had a secret to lure this elusive black ghost within
archery range. "A coffee can full of bacon grease". "Yes,
bacon grease". Scraps of meat were covered with logs
and a coffee can filled with grease was tied to a tree
off to the side. The reason for the can to be tied was
to prevent the bear from running off with its keep.
Every bear would head to the bacon grease first
before gorging the scraps of meat; sit on the
ground and lick all the grease out of the coffee
can. This gave ample time for a clear shot.

Near the shallow water's edge, many eels were concealed
under stones. Lifting one stone would sport half dozen
black slippery eels hiding from the day's sunlight.
The blood of an eel is very toxic to
humans and many animals.
This discourages creatures in the wild from eating them.
However, served cooked, eels are a delicacy to many people.
Italian and Asian restaurants serve this luscious
cuisine throughout the country.

Walking out onto a lumberjack trail stood this
moose twenty yards away staring at me.
Six to seven feet tall and nine hundred pounds of muscle
watching my every move, I was dumbfounded.
This animal looked like a prehistoric monster
you would see in the history books.

Once again, this virgin city boy's eyes are disbelief
of how large these animals could be.

Thinking back the many years how Native Americans lived
with hardships and perils of this great wilderness....
Respect was the primal obedience to the
bounds of nature to this beautiful land.

Speared

It is pitiful to write poetic creations about someone
and they will never read the pages full of life.

To beg for one's reflection for a cognitive
response is an underlying surface of truth.

Worthy of being loved is the most powerful
sensation provided from God.
Simple poetry is a relationship that we may grow or whither.

There are times I must commonly speak.
It is painful to remove the shards of glass from my
eyes, but I will keep writing until the day I die.

And when you read my thoughts,
I will not be here for your attention.

Reflected Skin

Leading through a lifetime, many torrents
of humanity pour against man.
Life becomes an ocean whistling and disappearing
with each wave bellowing currents across the land.

Argue with limitations they become yours.
The simplest questions are sometimes
the most difficult answers.
Why am I here?
To succeed is money really involved.
Where am I going?
What am I doing a minute from now?
What is love?

Watch within yourself how many times
the answers will change.
Divided lands become a problem because
we need a spiritual gift for reason.

Being true to oneself is a path to the
golden gate of inner prosperity.
True to others will never come, there will always be hypocrisy.

The Final Chapter

The smell of exhaust fumes permeating the air.
"Trees with no leaves".
Putrid grey limbs reaching out for help.

Progressive oxides, dioxides and mercury to an unending fate.
Defenseless nature choking to extinction beyond reason.

Is this all we know?
Smoke against the window, we don't care anymore.

Falling apart, we keep rotting our elegant
grace, granted from the heavens.

Build the inner dreams but stay inside the inner sphere.

A Soundless Journey

The next moon appeared
over the frosted meadow.
Slowly through the night,
delicate ice crystals pillowed
across the sky.

Far in a distant,
nature with no words,
perfect clouds,
wispy winds,
twist and spread
cotton fluffy waves
of blossom petals.

This gentle invitation
is a breathless beauty
to sooth the soul.

I do surrender
a rhythmic touch
to many wondrous
journeys.

I heard thy crisp winter voices.
Clear rich unpredictable winds,
magical as frosted diamonds
whisk in the sky.

Nature's leafless limbs
divulge a hundred winters
paralleled to life's mysteries.

The northern pines tossed their cones
to the song of the babbling brook.
This rhythmic sound echoed in the valley,
like the earth's howling wilderness,
gallant with mastery and force.

Shining through various pathways,
the sun produced a bluish orb
that pillowed deep
into this ancient forest.

The land fashioned
a heady perfume
with hypnotic spices
coveting the human mind.

From this unplanted forest dwelling,
where fallen acorns feed the deer, turkey, squirrel

and many more,
is God's blessing to the world.
62

We must understand the reason
behind his love,
and not destroy his gift
to the human man, woman and child.
We must protect for all eternity.

Crystal Crystals

The Blue Mountains mingle
with sapphire rivers.
Crystal springs,
cool polished stones glow
as the moon ignites the earth.

Stars stare with tears from lovers,
dancing dreams silhouette the sky.

Feathers feathered back,
sweeping diving
seeking nourishment,
a divine divinity
for courage to survive.

Roots flourish fingerlings,
bloom blossomed essence.
Mother Nature's nature,
cherish imaged images
naturally.

Felon

A simple flower
Unforgettable joy
Togetherness

A simple word
Eyes encountered
Aligns happiness

A simple dream
The moon
The stars
To see her smile

A simple thought
Love
Enchanting
Never ending

Nature Explodes

When nature explodes upon herself
The show is fast and exciting

The wind blows over like hungry dogs
Dramatic lighting and horrid thunder
Cracked trees from limbs to logs

The smell of burning ozone through the air
Gave us humans a tremendous scare

Children crying
Parents praying
Oh of God's power
Pour by the hour

Wishing the end soon to be near
For the sky to be sunny and clear

I send my love to my family and friends

From my heart

Please be safe
I pray for God's Grace.

The Coffee Shop

It's a beautiful life.
The streets may be icy.
They're not afraid to act
through the mist of the city.

Her lips grew sweet,
like the first spoon spilling sugar
into a creamy rich cup of coffee.
Pure emotion was guarded in this secret cup.

Studying each-other;
their instincts emulsified into a
passionate adoration propelled
against the vaulted sky.

Their words are a silent kindling,
burning rich in the garden of mystic embers.

Each glowing sparkle
wooed closer to that one.
That one kiss.

A man.
A woman.
For happiness guided by dreams.

Delicate softness.
Their first kiss completely absorbed into one.

To be someone that's never been.
Venus paralleled high above watching and
waiting for that second....... one.

Mystic Eternity

I love a woman who likes to hear every thought in my head.
I love a woman to spill her emotions to me.

Deep dark and ridiculous feelings
twisting our minds together,
establishing one meaning through artistic design.

Painfully different like the intense Arctic and Antarctic
poles, yet we are coupled with the Earth.
"A beloved Earth encircling the sun flowing with universe".

Watching that single star is a glowing brilliance
to our eyes, unquestionably there is love.

Poetry is intimacy we shared, where lips are soft,
gracious and gentle, spawning a mystic eternity.

A Test

A test,
carries truth,
carries lies,
within oneself.

To prosper,
is to a gallant heart
through selflessness.

Beauty is said to be through
the eyes of the beholder.
What is beauty?
What is the meaning of eyes?

A test of faith or is it called fate?
Faith is understanding unseen realities.
Fate is dealt with uncontrollable realities.
Are the two hand in hand?

Love!
Loved one-another.
A lost love.
Love thy self.
Love that never was.
Love you craved until the end of time.
Love that dies.

Hate!
To be destroyed a million ways,
Only one, consumed in today's war.
The war of hate!
The worst of all, not knowing.

A test.
A small complex trial with reality.
A lifespan unbeknown
to every living organism.

Winter's Bite

I freeze when the winter's blood touches my crumbling leaves.
Choking with each breath,
I wither under a canopy of brilliant white crystals.

When I'm alone,
I'm alone underfoot waiting with arms stretched to be held.

However with time, everything turns to a yellowish tint.
Covered in piss and contaminated with life's progress,
I'm sopping wet.
Rotting is inevitable, which becomes nothing.

The pizza delivery man is here!
Damn!
He slipped on the frozen yellow ice, breaking his back.
Another freaking lawsuit.

The earth runs through my hands.
The soil's soft rich deep fertile ground
envelopes patience and understanding.
This art of love finds tranquility's paradise
sprinkled with wildflowers.

Stars dancing in the moonlit sky,
tipping great oaks with subtle illuminations.

The world is our book.
Each page we expressed a cloaked feeling
hidden years in the shadow's abyss.

Each chapter encased a collection of
perceptions tantalizing the senses.
A gentle summer mist that clings softly to the skin.
A heart-pounding gaze into the stormy sea.
The delicate fragrance of honeysuckle blossoms
lured young lovers to lie in the fields. The
earth's magnificence is woven like a fine tapestry
into the many episodes of our lives.

Let the winds whisper for this gallant day.
Footsteps follow a gorgeous path bursting with
purple lilacs sweet and tasty full of life.
"A treasured kiss may all they seek".
Hypnotic euphoria freshened with desire
will emanate at this time and place.

And then at last,
as if compelled by the destiny that brought us together,
THE KISS. Soft, moist, gentle, seductive.

Her delicious, flavored spice,
swaying and clinging to my body.
Deep gentle moans hovering
the fleshy terrain, colliding into one.

A passionate rise as eagles soar and hearts
pound with a strong embrace,
the sweet kiss surrenders to a hungry desire
in the moments that will not be denied.

Nature's Hand

My arrowed fletch
pierced in rhythmic cadence.
Whispered through the air
In a softened reverence.

The slender wind waved a shadow less sigh,
tilting willows to the eastern side.

The nightingale sings
an hourly song.
His feathered wings
flutter along.

Nature's hand
open up
and carry my soul.
Deepened peace.
When it's real.
Not a forgotten jewel.

Let this arrow take me away.
Carry me with the wind.
Above the quiet earth
never to be seen again.

Matters

Washed dreams
quietly splintered.
Through poppy seed fields
life was in fear.
Does reality
really set it?

However.
Look far and near.
Peek around the corner
and see we are the lucky ones.

Wheelchairs,
blind,
deaf,
limbless,
sick,
homeless,
poor and starving.

The wretched feast on the weak.
Lies to the people.
Lies to ourselves.

Check the guest list,
see who's coming.

Opened eyes distinguish
guilt.
In a matter of minutes,
they drink their souls with the devil.
Happy New Year!

Pure Unsettled

Even in this twilight hour
you are like a divine orchestra
playing melodies with the stars.
Pure white statin laced angels
dance in glorious unison,
filling my heart with joy.

Reaching out with my fingertips,
I have fallen madly in love.
Touching this place you know,
it's in my blood to never let go.

So many times
we have kissed the morning star
to begin the new day.

I can't stop.
Let me.
Let me remember you.
I can't stop.
I can't let go.

Only if we were young again,
I would collapse in your arms.

Hands of Time

I have experimented
in life's uncut rules.

Searching an opening,
probing the universe.

By my own hands,
this journey devoured the flesh from my bones.

To flee from this caged monarch,
I was in battle with a haunting nuclei.

Like a twisted lace encircling my vocal cords,
I screamed without sound.

Torn between this madness.
Every scar I tried to hide
fell through the walls.

Hands of time revolved over and over,
until her fingers weaved into my wounds.

Holding on,
the knot got weak.
The soul was bound to break.

With a loss of health
and happiness,
our world will turn to dust.

Becoming extinct,
is how we forget to love.

Deserted Ways

I dare not beg for one last smile.
The demons rest in their insidious guile.

For I am lured to a ghastly test.
Within my tremulous pain,
I solely express.

Eroding melodies; rewording charm.
I fight to keep this man from harm.

Let the winds howl, fulminate, rave!
Protecting him from entering a deserted passing grave.

Awakening dreams were made to come true
Her curls will sense the midnight dew

Far in the heavens the galaxies converge
Layers her heart of spontaneous surge

Unfolding the pleasures that she'll pursue
Immortalized wonders of bountiful blue

To embrace the trinket of the moon's delight
Illuminates her beauty all through the night

Embrace the shadow, bind with chains.
Endure the power where righteous reigns!

Gazing At the Moon

Gazing at the moon,
she heard him from a distant
star.

At this twilight hour,
the indigo sky exploded
into poetic hallucinations.

However,
his calling did not touch her heart.
It appeared that a kiss sealed her voice
which paralyzed his soul.

Only a thousand poets
know the weight of his heart.
Do not write ridiculous poetry
concerning him.

There are many imperfections
in life's mysteries.
Piece together each star in our galaxy
to comfort reason.

Speechless in the loneliness of this hour,
life will go on like the mother-of-pearl
from their bodies.

I am twelve again,
smiling at my
first bedroom.

It's empty and ready
for my own bed.
Maybe a nightstand.
Maybe a dresser with a mirror.

Excitement was like I never felt.
A ten by ten room.
One hundred square feet.
All to my own.

Sleeping on the couch was okay.
I would watch and listen to the Nation
Anthem until the end of the day.

The morning was a little rough.
I would rise at the crack of dawn.
Eat breakfast, shower and run off.

I am twelve again.
How exciting!
I can't wait!
My own bed.
My own room.

No couch.
No living room.

I am twelve again.
I am one lucky kid
and thankful for this day.

The Devil is Loose

A lighted candle burns slowly
melting the divine hour of secrecy
where tortured souls lie in hell.
Sounding the iron bells,
thrusting into the necks of virgin gales.

Warlocks and witches sing through the night,
entertaining the devil with delight.

Beware what is what;
running on the loose
they'll find you;
squeezing, extracting
your eyes into juice.

When the midnight sky hovers over a dull grave,
fate smiles joy into death.
The recipe for burning thirst,
drink thy suffering bodies and eat their flesh.

They hide behind the concrete walls
peering through a millimeter crack.
Not sly.
Not smart.
A putrid musk mixed with fake smiles.
It's very easy to read the minds of superficial ignorance.
And to me,
shame for the chaos I've caused
in the sacred three.

A muse that struggles,
ebbs the tide.
From your sacred sphere,
look to the stars,
the tenderly bursts
are near the end.

A mirror can greatly hide the visible frowns.
My verse will peel the sickle from your hands.
A short-handled semicircular blade, used for
cutting, lopping the hearts of many.

Children's voices are blessed until they
listen to their fateful brood.
Outstretched hands are lined with silken
cloth shining down on this sphere.

Horror

Reality.
Boarded windows and doors.
Black and white force marked unambiguous
from a significant distance.

Escorted from schools,
They are lined up watching.
Ready to thrash the innocence of society.

One distinguished and honored human
assassinated,
terminated with extreme violence.

Stabbings go unnoticed on the streets,
in the bars and in schools.

With the sound of sirens, the night sky glows
a reddish color high in the night sky.

A young boy cannot understand the word hate.
Why in this beautiful world made from God's hands,
is being destroyed?

We were born to love and love back.
Born as nature feeds this world to survive.

Non-Hodgkin's

We talked and decided
Time for heaven
We are taken to her room
Tube down her throat
They inject high dosage of morphine
Then remove the tube
I see my mom gasp as I hold her hand
Oh my God
The pain I feel
The pain

Never have I experienced

The time is slow
Very slow
Until her last gasp
Now I see
The peace she is in
Calm and asleep

It's been over ten years
Today the treatment is unbelievable
People are surviving
They have hope

Heart of Cold

"You know who you are".
It's what invokes happiness
of lies.
Mindless wonders
between reality
and nothing.
Destroying the finest symbolic nature
to reasoned answers.
A toxic flavored pain;
burning the unsuspecting human.

Two faced pricks.
A death inside their heart.
A flea-market full of junk.

Church.
School.
Work.
Friends.
Whatever.

Spilling words out to display.
Your cold heart speared your reflected skin.
A soundless journey exploding pure unsettled lives.
The devil is loose, watching of men be the face of two.
All kinds.
"A trickledown effect".

in life,
did you ever
rewind?

look back,
wonder,
the one girl
you loved
and left.

a chapter in life
missing.
lost in the depth
of unchosen thought.
what would have
happened,
had you stayed?

in that young age.
love
made you real.

her eyes
lit up
the heavens.

her voice
calmed
the seas.

floating
on a cloud,
feeling her beauty,
was a verse
left
for a poem.

but yet,
life
wouldn't be
as today.

every season
will be
just a thought.

a memory
in
the wind.

a drop
of
fate.

Captured Beauty

Woman of my soul in sheer woven velvet
Knotted with lace that brushed her
skin like falling rose petals

A timeless and romantic fragrance following her every move
Captured beauty beyond the northern hemisphere

Shy as I was
I embraced what love has made
Walking through this endless garden of euphoria
What breathtaking gem she holds to her blossom of eternity

Her elegant posture turned to me
Encompassing an aura of such beauteous art
You've taken me to paradise

A Gentle Message

A gentle warm breeze called to her.
She heard a cardinal's note from the heavens,
a subtle flow of countless melodies.

"Your guardian angel to whom love commits,
gracefully comforts your soul".
This day may not be known,but
one love will never go.

"A gift has been given from the heavens".
Cloaked with golden wings from above,
your truth will never tarnish.

Thunder-clouds are wisdom, fierce and hot.
This test is true.
Amy, you are the sunshine with eyes to
survive when the days are gloomy.

Life of What Has Been Given

Emotions unleashed
Listen, open and exchange.
Somewhere under the promise land
there are dreams above dreams.

A lioness searches food through the
towering grasslands to survive.
Unknown of the future that lays ahead, her drive
is beyond what few humans will comprehend.

It's a collision of molecules unchanged and
unaffected going their own way.
At this moment in time, energy is life.

Unleash sacrifice is a true unknown enchantment for souls.
Sacrifice, like the soldiers who fight for
our country; dead and alive.

The Condor

The spit from a thousand ghosts haunt his virgin eyes.
Wrapped inside a blanketed nightmare, they
stood at the far corner of the bedroom wall.

Tears encased a stillness absorbing the
ugliness from a faceless body.

Lightning's clash with a rupturing
hailstorm burns the ozone's atoms.

Frozen limbs pulsating blood uncontrollably until
vomit spills madness from his young body.

Deranged humans destroyed the happiness from night's
pleasure.
Another sleepless existence will never vanish from innocence.

His Hands

95

A Dove
Never
Dies
In
The
Hands
Of God

Freudian Ghosts

There is a fear
that can drive
a human insane.

A desire to open up
a seductive taste
held deep within
a hidden circle.

Freudian ghosts
haunt this young man
for lost passion.

Life can change
one tenth of a second
or in eighty years.

We Are a Gift

I went to the forest,
then I went to the mountain.

Each place I sat alone
looking at the sky above.
A dark blue reflection surrounded
our planet's grace.

Two powerful pieces from God's creation.
A puzzle surrounded by living water.
A beauty that we all need to cherish.

Flesh from her floating lips,
infants born with fairytale stories
and golden paradise.

The old man in the mirror
sees his reflection with tears.
Once a upon a time,
nature ruled the world.
Virgin splendor unscathed by man.

Until.
Bulldozing.
Concrete.
Tar.
Blood.

Wars.
Murder.
What have we done?

The one gift.
The only gift to survive
is justice in our own hands.

I went to the forest,
then I went to the mountain.
I looked above the earth,
realizing we are a gift to nature.

Wondered Thoughts

Makes me wonder.
Spending days hiding down under.
Tell me your thoughts and dreams.

You're a lady of the stars.
Quiet as your heart shines.
Your level rays are like golden bars.
Spending days wondering,
will we keep this love inside.
With
thoughts of priority and pride.

Lady of the stars.

Makes me wonder.
Where beauty glows to make you smile.
Where dreams come true
and fill our hearts with joy.

Sometimes I sit on the highest cliff,
watching for that one star to cultivate beauty.
Unknown of color and shine,
my life becomes chance.

The Old Steel Mills

I sit here at 59 years old,
the show pissed away.
The mutilated world
chewed and spat out.

The terrible taste in my mouth
from the old steel mills
blown away.
Ash and dust are the last
remnants to stay.

Every morning the millions
of people traveling to survive.
"Look at their faces",
just starring through
a tunnel
planting seeds as they go on.

My right eye
Twitches uncontrollably
from all the stress,
from all the poverty,
from life.

Where are we going
in this free world?
"Cheers to this endless desire for sperm".
Keeps going and going.

The Gap Between Life

In between life there is a gap that few people know.
Imperfections are a clue where a soul does not deserve.

A dish cannot run away with the spoon,
only crack and salivate with germs.
Fairytales that warp the mind, implode violently inward.

We mention hope after there's pain.
Way before it was ever thought, Hope is
a figment to ease the human soul.
The question!
Who really cares before hope?

Destruction will always be,
That's life.
We were born behind obstacles of knowledge.
Let life flow into the ocean before it is drained.

Adam and Eve followed a lie.
Now existence is a speck of sand
in this desert we call earth.

Remember,
in between life there is gap.
Will it ever close?

Magic People

Are there magic people living on our planet?
Do these special people have a gift different
from any other living being?

I want to let it go.
Could I show the pain
from the magic
I can't hold on to me.

What's locked inside of me,
I can't be freed.
Never wanted to be so cold.
Will magic let me go?

My darkest is unknown.
Will I be forever alone?

To look inside,
you need a key.
But the key is lost
in depths of a broken mind.

I have nothing left;
all I feel is a burden
to love that never was.

The Night in Atlanta

I want to get to know your body without you undressing.
I was looking in my dreams when I saw you.
In a mysterious way I was consumed.

The heat stripped me naked.
The traffic outside my window kept going.
Not one single soul had any knowledge I was naked.
They kept busy screaming and honking
their horns at each other.

It was Atlanta.
An average class hotel.
The weather seasonably hot.
At a hundred and twenty dollars a night;
the air conditioned room had a poor billowing
source of comfort.

We talked on the phone.
Her voice close as ever.
Pure,
sweet and somewhat exuberant.
This was her style.

What's inside of us is a beautiful dream.
The moon said we are an open book,
everything will happen like the pull of gravity.

We will make love
as the solar winds carry us to an
uncharted solar system.
I'll breathe the fragrance of her soul.

The traffic outside my window kept going.
I was still naked.

I know who she is.
Irresistible as a wild
crystal diamond.

A spirit that conceived me,made
from flesh.
A physical art in full bloom.
Pure crimson lace
wrapped around my naked body,
I wait.

I wait like a clover lost
in a thunderstorm,
drenched with tears,
imprisoned from dreams.

I stumble across a flickering light.
Am I this ghost in a dimension
inflamed with nakedness
that's transparent?

Love can't be told,
it's hidden in my veins.
Bluish as evening sky,
I bleed internally.

We Made Love

In Paris we made love.
The cathedrals where silent.
Le Mar Des Je t'aime nestled in the petit garden square.
Walking the pure century old cobble-stone streets, the
ethereal beauty glistened from the lunar moon.
In the mist of France we were unstoppable.
Our climax fashioned human desire.
We screamed the comfort of ecstasy.
Shadows silhouette the walls showing two bodies intertwined.

In Venice we made love.
A gondola ride for two.
We passed flamboyant mystic buildings.
A kiss beyond a thread of grace.
Romantic lips inescapable,
flesh desire flesh.

In Spain we made love.
A journey into undiscovered charm,
revealed passion's romantic secrets.
Barcelona captivated beautiful harmonies of the heart's sea.
Making love was an art of eternity.
Our cream passed with intensity, immersed into
a treasure sweet as a book of love poems.

We made love in California, Pennsylvania,
Montreal all over the world.

I am thankful with this dazzling night of dreams.
Will she read my dream?

On a Path

I tried to be a perfect gentleman,
and this word called "love" ripped my heart.
I was chosen to be the broken stone to lies.

Lies that crumbled dreams to dust.
From a pure crystal spring,
I was carried to depths of the Nile River.
Dark, dank mud.
A mixture of soil,
sludge, and poison.

The bright sun reflects a brown glow
to the empire.
This germ infested flow will carry me to the open sea.

The Mediterranean carries opened dreams to become alive.
Blue turquoise rising to your iris.
A refection for my dreams to awaken.
Pure passionate desire warms my heart.
I feel alive.

First Breath

Kissing a woman is the greatest honor.
To love a woman and for her to return love back,
radiates like the born of spring-life
taking her first breath.

Straight from the sun,
light plunges warmth below the clouds.
Love rises with hunger,
as hunger rises with love.

He's still waiting with his wine
and a dance cheek to cheek.
A passionate lover becomes the beggar,
the beggar pleads to meet.

The Burning Forest

I think of you all the time.
My wisdom is lost in the gallows of love.
Loneliness was created by a fool.
Without loneliness, I could not be created.
I wrote for love, but I love in secrecy.

I'm the burning forest that was ignited
with one ignorant match
lit from a stranger's cigarette.
Everything in it's path turns to ash.
All is gone, never again to be replaced.

Her picture is my soul.
A longing that was cloaked by words
only I shall know.
Woman,
eyes of blue,
I dreamt life was beautiful dancing in your arms.
I'm crazy for that one kiss.

To think my path is closing to the end.
My seizures have a power to scalp the mind.
Am I angry?
Am I lost?
My fear is filled with desire to open the skies.
A fantasy to know your mine.

One summer's night I had a dream.
Deep into an unawaken soul,
I was begging to be freed.
I tried to discover my identity.
I was lost.

Then a beautiful woman appeared under the stars.
Quaint, quiet and soft.

Long silken hair glowing with the universe.
Harmonizing
a peaceful serenity
gliding across the midnight sky.

Her delicious perfume scent,
an exhilarating utopia,
bathed the air.

Succulent,
simmering,
endless rapture.
Petals in bloom.

I awake.

Tears Encased

Where dawns dusk consumes twilights to a wishers dream,
he fell silent.

Her tears were secretly encased,
flowing through a marble elliptic hourglass,
waiting endlessly to disappear.

His delicate crystals stand abroad a blue-green horizon,
praying that one day her struggles will escape.

It's a lonely world of frightened lovers.
Fairytales are caged, screaming to unleash
a rose that makes the dead beautiful.

Like a single feather guided with the wind.
Happenings are just.

Reaching out where blossoms bloom is
a step where birds will sing.
That first kiss is waiting.

Rescue Me

I fell in love with an angel
You opened my heart
Kiss me
Wanting
Waiting for you
Eyes like a feather
All the love I seek to be
I pray your heart will fall for me
My life was like a dream
I believed you would rescue me
You gave me hope and kept me out of misery
I fell in love with an angel
Eyes like a feather
Nothing can decide, it was what I believed
You can rescue me
Angel of light
You stole my heart

Absorbing Grace

Distraction.
Illusion.
Delusion.
Replenish the mind.
Pull from what really matters.
To what life?
To what scene?
Ask and don't tell.

To live without tasting the water's essence,
a tempest surge adrift mocking sails,
are guided blindly through a bog of locked reason.

The images are there to explore.
Patiently we choose to learn secrets
that are wild and bewildering.

Sometimes we sit on the ocean's bottom,
waiting for that one oyster to cultivate beauty.
Unknown of color and texture,
our quest becomes chance.

Inverted shadows flock with the moon's rays,
hovering over our eternal beauty.
To the silent one,
life is absorbing yesteryear's grace.

This state of consciousness,
is the inner vision through gatherings,
to replenish the spirit and body.

After centuries, the golden gates were finally opened.
Known as:
"The keeper of keys"
St. Peter appeared with a glowing smile.

Single file waiting their turn to enter the Kingdom of God,
millions of the deceased were praying their penance.

Walking through the crowd,
St. Peter crossed a stream where babies and the unborn wait.
Slowly St. Peter raised his arms calling out.
"Your father is waiting for you"
St. Peter cradled every soul.

Reaching to the gates,
St. Peter turned to the crowd and said welcome.

Devour me in a gentle manner.
Let the winds carry us to where the mountain meets the sea.

I tremble thinking in brief.
The cliffs are there waiting.
Love had a way and falling was a beautiful madness.

The insanity to think when our naked
skin devoured each other,
I was at a loss.
Her head rested on my chest.
I watched every breath, ending in a soft sigh until sleep.

A single tear fell down my cheek reminding me what is.
Yet the bliss of heaven,
the flowers of spring and the fragrance in bloom,
all rest in my arms at this minute in time.
Where time has stopped to another world.
I tremble.
I watch.
I cannot let go.

Death is a little thing created by God.
Silently suffocating in a rhythmic fashion,
my heart is bursting to love.
A love that will never become.

I whispered to the sky asking to end this entombed devotion.
Bury my soul like a madman, quietly choosing destruction.
This is my magnificent insanity to love.

OUR MIND, OUR BODY, OUR SOUL
Petals from a rosebush form a rose,
but the roots give life to its beauty.
So what's underneath the dark soil that can't be seen?
Balanced nutrients of complex substances,
provides the essence to survive.

Understanding these words is the law of the earth.

Impulse

When we were alone
under a spruce tree,
the clouds seemed not to move
and yet the winds whispered
to us in privacy.

What was impossible became possible,
we kissed.
Her floating romantic scent
mixed with wild earthen pine,
smelled sharp,
sweet and refreshing.

There was a long silence,
I surrendered to her art.
I witnessed love,
dreams and pain.
No one. ... no one will ever discover
how astonishing we were.

Impulses fell
into a pure transformation
beyond the mystical universe.
In her glow,
I learned to love.
In her words,
I sacrificed all things.
She was Venus, I was Mars.

Fragile

I was in love with a vision knowing I met her.
I was searching while she escaped
from her past;
a nightmare.

I called,
she answered.
A fragile voice whispered under the stars.
In this circle,
here lies a secret.
"Before the heavens,
 open what's been closed for decades".

Let us be young again,
 chase each other across a field of buttercups.
We will calm the hectic winds,
 drink the world's beauty.
Share our reflection from the sun's rays.

My eyes beg to see your smile.
My lips beg for your kiss.
Your fragrance drives me wild,
like a lioness seducing her king.

Curtained behind life's hectic world.
Loving you,
I know not any other way.

Of all the many poems.
I write this poem for you.
Under breath,
in silence,
where dreams will never end.

In the space of solitude,
the mind lives to venture without permission.

Only one answer.
Three words.
I plead to know.

The Moment I Looked Into Her Eyes

Some of the most internal battles are dealing with love.
A love that is unlikely to happen.
A love that may only exist for one.
For many, it can be sad.
For few, they may be blessed.

That moment we looked at each other,
my eyes fell onto her eyes.
Delightful and enchanting, she was beautiful.
Like the moon reflecting off the ocean,
with glowing patterns so tranquil my body
collapsed revealing a weakness.

However, it wasn't the pearl that furled my wings.
It was the golden rose from inside her heart,
that absorbed my soul.

To hear her voice,
as a simple hello.
Soothing and quiet,
touched the moment of time.
At least for that moment,
she made me feel alive.
Regardless of what's being said,
I was delighted to listen.

Does her lips feel soft with a kiss.
Pure, delicate, delicious, adorable.
I wonder if heaven exists.

Right before she goes to sleep,
is there a thought?
Love may never be known,
or do I really want to know?
I'm....in heaven....
I will love her in my heart.

The body of a rose,
transient form unto a timeless uncleaned
crustacean organism.

Her mysterious past hidden in a non-fiction novel,
festering wounds open from a deranged psychotic mind.
Dead babies searching for their soul.

Nothingness to the profanity spilt from his lips,
misery has finally fell from grace. He is worn.

Annie sledged the bones built to journey
through an odyssey of manuscripts.
Rise to a new beginning of terror.
A walking winter wonder land falls to spring.
A spring of hell.
Manuscript!
Manuscript!
She must live!
Unsuspecting letters turn into blood and a desperate tear.
Blue tulips burst through the melting snow.
Between life and life.
There is will to survive.

The finale!
Drinking the champagne from her filthy distorted hands.
A toast to the heir.

One strike.

Eat it you sick twisted "f".

In the end the final word is typed.

Oh Paul!

I'm sorry for the people I've hurt, but
I'm not sorry for my dreams.

Loneliness is a stigmatic possession dealing
with horrors concealed in oneself.

A crisis that can cut across your heart.
Unaware from the slow trickle of blood
pouring into the atmosphere,
befitting a slow death.

We can smile and laugh.
Dance and sing.
Exercise until the body drops.

It's clear.
You can hide.
Even the brightest medical doctors
will never know.

No rhyming.
No rhythm.
It's simple.
An empty living soul.

Loneliness screams to become free.

Stay busy and everything will be forgotten.
Remember there is always someone worse than you.

Penetrating His Ripened Body

Distance has ways to open or close your heart.
The Country:
The Inn:
The Suite:
After a long delay, the impending challenge was revealed.
Succulent energy balanced between euphoria
and tranquility was real.

Everything and nothing has spoken.
Her aromatic scent penetrated his ripened
body, excepting no return.
Breath into breath,
fluent dipping of tongues,
pairing the fruit's nectar.

Her breast flush against his lips.
The flesh;
pink delicious,
creamy and fresh.

Edible,
sweet thighs and warm
mouth-watering flavor,
like salted caramel dripping luscious syrup
from a hot roasted apple.
Running down her skin,
as if his lips were made for poetry.

Shaking, sweating, wet.
Dancing in the shadows, in front of his eyes.
She begins to scream with eloquent thirst.
Je veux faire l'amour avec toi!
Je veux faire l'amour avec toi!

I want to make love with you!

Flames above the crimson sky don't ever stop.

"A flower; no matter where it blooms
 there is beauty within our vision".

Echoes in My Heart

Retracing the path back,
lifting the abstruse vocalization.
There we were under the vaulted posada,
enthralled by unexplained reasoning.

The echoes continue to haunt my life cycle,
playing within the spirit's cognitive artery.
Juliet;
as I begin to feel you inside me,
each seed embedded the taste of honey.

We were eye level when your voice cried "I love you"!
In no doubt,
my response "I love you"!

The hidden photos are eloquent.
A chest of memories.
A treasure instilled held only by thread.

Love will not falter from my last breath.
What we made inside,
my life blood red.
I opened your soul to new.
A nocturnal sphere held tight
a life of blue.

Your last words.
Destruction beyond worlds.
What echoes in my heart?
Again, "I love you".

A Robin's Egg

Society makes it hard to love like it once was.
The depths beyond has fallen to this world of ignorance.
Yes! Blame, argue, lie.
A rat race between oneself.
A "Dropbox" leading through a tunnel of emptiness.
Omissions and commissions find fault.

Feelings come and go like thunder during a
midnight storm, rolling over and under.
Uttering words to hurt without thoughtful compassion.

Show that you understand.
Embrace those you love and don't love.
Set your heart on good.
Reasoning is what truly matters.
Doing it over and over again with mistakes is truth.
Learn to praise others.
From all this, we are born to love.

I watched a robin build a nest.
Within days there where eggs.
Every night she kept the eggs warm.
Than one day, nature's wonders unlocked.
Three chicks lay side by side.
Every day the male and female fed their babies.
The chicks grew one by one.
Feathers and all.
They were gone.
Is this nature's love?
Maybe we all should learn from this.

Delicious Violets

The moon spilled onto the earth, overwhelming
the stars soaked in sleep.

Let the wind's curiosity make love in the Garden of
Eden where violets grow untouched by human hands.

Reveal the luminosity and rhythmic
wings of magnificent insanity.
The gentle moans.
The piercing screams.
Fruit is ripening for that exotic flavor;
delicious to the lips.

Thirsty for the thighs,
crashing against the howling flesh.
Unstoppable lightning exploded in the darkness.
Lost in time,
nothing will ever be this beautiful again.

Barriers

My heart is weary, but there was one
and only one feeling you left in response.
May this be a well treasured
keepsake forever I hold.
Does love exist behind barriers?

Our First Glass

I can feel your pulse escalate.
In this art of seduction;
yes,
oh yes.

Of course we were young,
but I looked back into the years,
gazed at the world;
until,
until our lips brushed neatly coating each other's skin.

Pulling close,
we danced before our hearts exploded.
Collapsing on the bed was what we desired.
Distance had no barriers and what carried through
is incomparable to "it just happened".

Making love was everything we desired.
A kiss; your smell; melted me into you.
My fingers tight as a crimson vine around your waist.
Gradually absorbing passion's moisture,
driving instinctively nature's romantic temple.

In this vast world, love surged like a stupendous
sea crashing the cliffs of Moher.

Savoring our first glass,
my eyes saw what my hands
sensed.

Heart in Battle

There was a day when the wind was so cold
And her heart was so bold
Hatred poured out of her mouth
A word that I never learned
Her story never heard

The kind of things that aren't meant to explain
What remains behind is vain
Are the ones you hurt in pain

Where her thoughts can hide
One day, her eyes will open wide
And
God will remember her and feed her the love inside

Stridulous Call

Winter is not yet gone,
but the trees cascade a fragrance
summoning life to be awakened

The wind with a stridulous piercing call
begins to whip around the mountains
amidst a cunning smile

While the rain breaks against the ice,
streams become rivers
A pathway for the galloping sediment will flow
feeding the earth's creation

Above the clouds,
the sky is animated with mallards
returning to mate and begin a new family
The leader guides his flock to a paradise for safe haven

Nature's piece will flow once again
with the energy from our planet's life cause

Hidden In the Breeze

With my eyes
I can feel her steal me away
Long draws underlay a quivering fever
Consuming desire in the night

Tenderly her lips placed onto mine
A few light kisses we embraced
A breath in fragrance between nature and our bodies,
we unclothed in the shadows of pines

We exist to whom we are,
limitless as the needles fall from an evergreen

In the midst of the warm thermals,
her body's ever changing scent climaxed
with a wardrobe of kisses

Hardened by passion,
our trembling thirst is ripe
and fruitful

With no words only a smile,
there is an infinite love hidden in the breeze

A Hint of Lavender

Come my sweet,
unlace your scarlet beauty
My calloused hands
are just one thread from a pillowy cloud

Listen to the wind from the mountain top
Let our naked bodies touch the hidden stars

A hint of lavender touched the breeze
The thermals rose with your lasting scent

A sky lit fragrance absorbed
our intoxicating thirst
The breathing intensified
as my lips pressed against your neck

The northern lights cast
a blue-green
purple-pink
glow from your eyes
I shall not resist
making love to you

Let's escape where eagles fly
A quiet place
Far away

A Trickle of Water

I gave my life to the forest
An ageless beauty
A solemn melody
Fermenting leaves
Where angels speak to the wilderness of hidden secrets

Clean intoxicating aroma of pine trees saturate the air
Wild-flowers unfold their petals
Bees harvesting nectar

A trickle of water flows into a stagnant pond
filled with tadpoles waiting to transform
Creatures frolicking in their natural paradise
is a reason for heaven's shore

Cradling my heart is a drunken overflow of Eden's power
An eternal passage to the trumpet's
encounter

Grapes to Wine

Body covered in mud but with a tranquil smile.
Her arms held grapes to make Moscato wine.
The money she earns are pennies to a dime.

Morning until night,
women harvest from the healthiest vine.
Only the finest wines are prepared for the wealthiest lives.

Grapes to glass captivate a rich man's taste.
Cheers to the free world as arms embrace.

Late that night.
In a city booming of street-lights and bars.
A young man and his bride were walking,
gazing at the stars.

From around the corner
a toddler appeared.
With his arms reaching out
he had no fear.

Tagging along like a lost puppy dog.
This couple understands the final epilogue.

A little disturbing and not knowing what to do.
"I turned to the boy and gave him my food"

Like shadows from a cloud.
"Gone in seconds"
He takes the bag and runs off into the crowd.

Tired from a long day,
the couple retreat to their hotel.
Walking back,
they peer around the corner to see a woman
crouched down with her baby eating their meal.

This woman from the fields looked up and smiled.

Covenant

Ancient blossoms,
mortal souls,
bloom in the candescent light

Sacred breath,
caressing lips,
embracing a blissful night

A kiss is captivating,
sealed with a covenant passion
More precious than gold
and a sweet taste of obsession

Shall we confess this gentle touch,
seeks to drink from mouth to mouth.

Tasting the oils from her hidden jewel,
patience my queen we'll stay in control

To live in harmony
    One breath is life's eternity

Imprisoned

From Adam's rib to Eve.
A coiled sword tempered in blood scored her skin.

Pink petals under a heavy fog pummeled the earth.

Wolves clean the meat of a carcass,
leaving bones for the mice and moles.

What's this all have to do?
It's love that I miss,
that's ripping my flesh.

In all complexities of the night,
my imprisoned lips are alone.

Nerves on nerves,
I cried for an answer.

Out of the pit,
poised like an angel
and teeth of a vole.
Madness reigned.

The garden was closed.

Could you tell?
It hurts.
A kiss may never be.
Never again.

Devil's Tongue

Yesterday's vicious hour,
    claimed destruction on the innocent.
Caught in the fire of bloodshed,
    time was broken.

The devil's tongue called out to deliver
devastation on the young.
Unknowingly their dreams were stolen.

A measured bullet slicing through the
air was calculated to kill.
Staring eyes become a burning cigarette
from an infectious man.

His broken shell consumed evil over good.
The maggots thrived on human chaos until the end.

Impulsive bureaucracies received a unanimous decision. A
child bent over pleading his presentation,
    fell to his knees and broke.

Rage and prayers,
    but nobody listens.

In a seedless light,
    how many more will perish?

Trumpeter's Encounter

I gave my life to the forest
An ageless beauty
A solemn melody
Fermenting leaves
Where angels speak to the wilderness of hidden secrets

Clean intoxicating aroma of pine trees saturate the air
Wild-flowers unfold their petals
Bees harvesting nectar

A trickle of water flows into a stagnant pond
filled with tadpoles waiting to transform
Creatures frolicking in their natural paradise
is a reason for heaven's shore

Cradling my heart is a drunken overflow of Eden's power
An eternal passage to the trumpeter's
encounter

The Fiddler's Way

She sat in a costume of white and golden silk.
Cultivating the council until the madness spilt.

Under a smile in the most seductive way.
The edge of her blade shall not betray.

Propositioning.
Violating.
Confusing the mime.
The jester's fiddle made music to the mind.

Viciously seductive,
her scent roamed through the palace.
With amusement,
the king welcomed her to drink from the sacred chalice.

Word spread like wildfire.
Our majesty and the joker where sleeping in bed.
The duke called for the queen.
She responded.
Off with their heads!

The queen raised her prize high in the air
and the knights called out dilly! dilly!
Let's drink a beer.

Climbing the Stem

Color the earth.
Grow from the roots.
Climb the stem.
Kiss the heavens.

A mother's child.
Nurture the body.
Path to peace.
Rise to bloom.

Hummingbirds cry.
A call for nectar.
The recipe for life.
One day we wilt.

Rehearse the lines
to unmask the mortal.
Call the thunder
and wake your pulse.

In this world.
Let it out.
Let it leave.
There's no blaming
when you look in the mirror.

Silent Taste

The leaves tried to imitate his hands by
embracing her body falling from the sky.
Above the forest floor the wind buffered
the woman's enticing cry.

How do you plead for love that was
lost in a forgotten wilderness?
With a gentle glance he entangled the vines of weakness.

Living far between the mountains where ballads are spoken,
the moonlit songs were kept precious and unbroken.

Every taste from their lips was filled with endless fruit.
Their silent dream of love harmonized an everlasting truth.

Entangled Vines

The leaves tried to imitate his hands by
embracing her body falling from the sky.
Above the forest floor the wind buffered
the woman's enticing cry.
With a silent glance he entangled the vines of weakness.

Squeezing the Leaves

I held her naked body,
caressing softly with my lips.

Tasting innocence,
she arched her back,
welcoming a desire she had never known.

I loved her with a force causing her legs to tremble.
Filling the sky with moans we had to quiet our rapture.

Yet the steaming pleasant aroma soothed the air,
increased passion and romance.

She was crying my name with desire,
like petals sprouting from a rose screaming for sunlight.

Squeezing the leaves
and soil between our fingers
we lost control.

Unforgettable hours of making love.
Sweat poured down onto her.
Taking seduction with temptation nice and easy,
we made it right.

Memories are like a resolution;
they can aim for hope or
shoot you through the heart.
What can be destroyed completely,
is not easy for one to depart.

Like a drop of honey in hot tea,
give yourself up without affliction
and in exchange
taste honor in humility.

Essential joy that is devoted into drinking,
you can smell honey or tea
mixed for spiritual healing.

The sacred stirring bestows a golden blend
of hope for the unfortunate.
In time,
this will promote wisdom for a sullen fate.

The softness of a pillow is not from the shell,
it's the feathers of sacrifice that keeps you from hell.

Cockled into a deep rumination.
Plagued by thoughts and
spilled into a darkened room.
She cries to escape.

Her mind is an enemy
manifested by reality and insanity.
Listening to the recording of lepers wailing.
She begins to go mad.

It often happens when waiting in the darkness
where promises are made and never kept.

Like rungs on a ladder,
each step is chosen to escape
from the agonizing soul in exile.
Unaware the last step may be the end,
she takes her chance. Her only chance.

You are the reason for hope
All I am is a poem
to surrender the love that is present in your heart

Cultivate the seed that will sprout to the universe
My words are a simple gesture
that whispers in the wind

The unexplainable is a drizzle
undetected by will

What love has taught,
color me into your dream
and
hold me until you sleep

Sometimes you become so use to emptiness,
you forget about reason.
It's a transparent and artificial death.

This illness will hide your face,
your eyes and beneath your heart.
And when it hurts you feel the burning madness of confusion.

Opinion can ruin a soul if obscured wisdom is borrowed.
Be oneself and act naturally on your own instinct.

The mind resembles an hourglass.
All the ideas we experience are collected,
tested and refined.

Educated reason for humility
so they can understand what life's
expectancies are required for the Way.

Let her heart wait until it fills with light,
and the "Way" we achieve harmony and riches
is to unite with the body.

No wine will ever become grapes.
No paper will ever become a tree.

The wooden rafters will shake during a windy storm
as you write a letter to your love.
A love that was never.

Drink the wine to celebrate life.
Be ready for change.
Come here with no shame.
His lips have forgotten the sweet taste of desire.

Ecstasy is flooding their soul as the spring fills the river.
Torrential rapids explore each other's pleasure zone
until it explodes.

Appreciate the embedded romance that has been unearthed
and explore sensuality.
Each are both a melting mystery.

However,
is it really foolish if you miss the reality of bliss?

Through the black-forest hills in search of his hidden stand.
She traveled with her hunter to a timeless land.

Guided by a glow under a canvas of stars.
Peering high in the sky they discovered the red planet Mars.

Through a sweet earthen fragrance mixed with a misty dew,
they walked the clandestine trail where
there's always something new.

Restless oaks towering over the aspen,
a soul's paradise for folks to imagine.

You feel the cleansing of each breath.
You hear nature at her best.

You see the flowing secrets from God.
You taste the air of soil and sod.

Yes, the science and art will be put to a test.
We'll know if this archer's skill will be at its best.

They climb the stand that's twenty feet high.
This is her first time to peer from the sky.

Scanning the terrain ahead and to the sides,
she's amazed on how the country's
ridge-tops and valleys reside.

With daylight the thermals rise.
You know that each tree has a unique surprise.

The pines having a sweet calming effect
and the moist fallen leaves permeate as the collect.

What happiness can there be other than the
conversation with individuality?
Only the harvest of a high spirituality.

Eyes Are Watching

The hawk's screech alarms its prey.
The victim becomes still....
in search of a sanctuary.

Like birth, cuddle as a lamb,
for warmth and safety.

The end can be near.
Lessons learned....
is inevitable to survive
in the wild.

One chance,
or a reluctant mind
may cease.

Attainment is a process
of experience.
Be one with yourself.
Concealment is crucial
to living a prosperous life.

In all,
tomorrow will be new day
for existence.

Each Arrow Destined

I have briefly forgotten to understand
the responsibilities of love.

Merciless patience has distanced my soul.

My veins have cleaved their way into a far off journey
beyond a methodical course.

Flesh that was always held in a utilitarian view
has broken into an unethical justice.

Each arrow held in the quiver carries its own direction.

Only from the guidance of the bow and
archer will predict their destiny.

Tethered

Behind the stillness horizon,
blemished mortals seek the fletch tipped arrow
with wings.

Inside the realm of God,
life is an unforgettable journey
to survive.

Nickel Plated

Chained to the floor,
the mob staggered back in from the wind.
Motionless the vipers slithered extending their fangs.

Placing the six gun on his lap,
the nickel-plated, thirty two revolver
never transfixed,
but dead on the flesh it kicks.

Now the prism's refractive surface is distorted.
The trajectory and smoke descended in the distance.

The humanity is expected,
"Eff-off" with a vengeful bitter agony.

Wired webbed windows shattered in the night.
The neon sign kept blinking bright.

The lantern blazed in itself.
Limiting a cast upon the wall.

These bright boys of outlaws are disciples.
Exploring the streets to survive.

Intoxicating Passion

As the earth time changed in early spring.

Somewhere now he stands, steam pouring from his body.
Heat and humidity screaming, but no breeze.

Her pulsating heart crossed over with trembling hands.

This hysteria is an intoxicating passion wrapped
around their delirious emotions.

To the lips of forgotten fruit,
let them pass between rivers,
moistened for thirst of a delicate star.

Their hidden grace 'neath lace unraveled
by the rosebud's thorn.
And when they transcend, petals unveil in a storm.

Eclipsed by Eros's shadow.
A pervasive zephyr begins to burnish their flesh
like pearls refracted through glass.

A love completely spontaneous and uninhabited absorption.
Followed by a perfumed fragrance,
life's consummation has been fulfilled.

A Mother's Whisper

Hovering beyond the heavens
there was a moment,
when the crisp spring morning
culminated over a painted horizon

In awe
This emerald splendor saturated by our mother's display
Whispered sweet innocence amidst the month of May

Perched high on an oak the Purple Martin sings
Enchanting melodies and gracefulness
this delightful bird brings

The mourning doves coo with a soft
caressA secret elation they only possess

Westerly winds are tailored to the entwining land
and where secrets behold from her tender hands

This tapestry is woven into an earthly slumber
Where inquisitive spirits are born to wonder

Nature's benediction could be heard
from her murmuring voice
Pursuing divinity is a glorious rejoice

About the Stories

The Oil Field:

is an authentic story living in Hazelwood, Pittsburgh Pennsylvania. The names have been changed to protect the privacy of individuals.

Legend of the Razor Back:

is an authentic story in Hazelwood, Pittsburgh Pennsylvania. The names have been changed to protect the privacy of individuals.

Electric Street:

is an authentic story in Hazelwood, Pittsburgh Pennsylvania. The names have been changed to protect the privacy of individuals.

Thunder under the Sky:

is an authentic story located in Washington Pennsylvania.

Pittsburgh Pirates:

is a combination of a fictional and authentic story. The names have been changed to protect the privacy of individuals.

Dinner Time for Spider: a poem on All Poetry.

The Alley:

combination of a fictional and authentic story. The names have been changed to protect the privacy of individuals.

The Green Cadillac: fictional story.

Grapes to Wine:

is a poem for the prompt: "Keep the Ones who Heard you When You Never said a Word"..... J.York

A Mother's Nightmare:

is an authentic story posted on All Poetry. The names have been changed to protect the privacy of individuals.

The Forest:

is combination of a fictional and authentic story in Quebec Canada. The names have been changed to protect the privacy of individuals.

Speared:

is a poetic write for the All Poetry. Into the darkness picture prompt.

Reflected Skin:

is a poem for All Poetry "Twisted Tuesdays presents the artwork of Emanuele Dascanio".

The Final Chapter: Write on anything.

A Soundless Journey:

is a poem for prompt, "Snow falling soundlessly in the
middle of the night will always fill my heart with sweet clarity"
— Novala Takemoto

Crystal Crystals: prompt "Nature's Nod".

Felon: write for a friend.

Nature Explode:

picture prompt for a "Fluffy airborne seed of a dandelion".

The Coffee Shop:

prompt quote, "How strange it is to fall in love with a
complete stranger, but how even more strange it is the moment
as if you've known them your entire life" Mason Flower.

Mystic Eternity:

prompt "The Artwork of Loui Jover......It's Written On Her Face".

Winter's Bite:

prompt "The snow doesn't give a soft white damn whom it
touches." — E.E. Cummings

A Path to Paradise:

Art of Seduction—Pablo Neruda
Quote
""""I crave your mouth, your voice, your hair... """" ~Pablo
Neruda, translated from Spanish by Stephen Tapscott

Nature's Hand:
"A Slender Wind" Dylan Thomas: THE DEVIL'S
PLAYGROUND THE POEM—SHADOWIN

Deserted Ways:
"If you start to miss me, remember. I didn't walk away.
Youwalked away".

Gazing at the Moon:
"New Year—a new chapter, new verse, or just the same old
story? Ultimately, we write it. The choice is ours."

Looking Back:
Thanksgiving and Poetry.

The Devil is Loose: The Mortuary of Shadows.

One Can Be the Face of Two: "Winter of our Discontent".

Horror: "Sultry Saturday Halloween Special!!!".

Non-Hodgkin's: "Disease".

Heart of Cold: "Must contain word cold".

A Drop of Fate:
"Memory is man's greatest friend and worst enemy."
~ Gilbert Parker

Captured Beauty: "The word Nothing".

A Gentle Message: "Convey words of encouragement"

Pen heartfelt lines~

Life of What Has Been Given:
"It is precisely our recognition of life's inevitable hardships, along with our uprooting of the attachment that exacerbates them, that allows us to appreciate the mere fact of being. -Reverend Patti Nakai.

The Condor: "Dragons-roam".

Freudian Ghosts:
"Fear closes his eyes as courage wakes the fight".

We Are a Gift: "Quick fire on life".

Wondered Thoughts: "Falling Stars".

The Old Steel Mills:
"Boring damned people, all over the earth. Propagation more boring damned. What a horror show. The earth swarmed with them.
~ CHARLES BUKOWSKI

Internally:
"Long after I have given up, my heart still searches for you ... without my permission" — Rudy Francisco.

We Made Love:
"Making you horny and making you smile are my two favorite things". ~ Shivam Chandak

First Breath: "You are my Happy"

The Burning Forest:
"Wish I didn't miss you"! — Angie Stone

Tears Encased:
"dawns dusk consumes twilights to a wishers dream".

It's a Lonely World of Frightened Lovers:
"Have you ever lived dead inside until day of the dead awakes
with life's lips".

Absorbing Grace:
"My yesterday's walk with me. They keep step, they are gray
faces that peer over my shoulder." ~ `William Golding

Carry Me to an Endless World:
"I hate that ... I love you". –Lyrics by gnash

The Moment I Looked Into Her Eyes: "I Think of You"

Number One Fan: "Horror".

Penetrating His Ripened Body:
"Where There's Smoke There's Fire".

A Robin's Egg:
"Define your thoughts on society today".

Delicious Violets:
"I only believe in intoxication" ... — Anais Nin

Our First Glass:
"Follow your inner moonlight, don't hide the madness."
~~ Ginsberg Quote

Stridulous Call: "Nature's Interactions"

Hidden in the Breeze: "What a Lovely Way to Burn".

Grapes to Wine:
"Keep the Ones who Heard you When You Never said a
Word""... J.York

Covenant:
"Ancient Lovers believed a kiss would literally unite their
souls, because the spirit was said to be carried in one's
breath."... Eva Gicksman

Devil's Tongue: "School Shooting"

Trumpeter's Encounter:
Use the word "Stagnant".

The Fiddler's Way: "Jesters and clowns".

Silent Taste:
"Golden slumber kiss your eyes; Smiles awake you when you
rise" ""– Thomas Dekker

A Sullen Fate:
"Memories are bullets. Some whiz by and only spook you.
Others tear you open and leave you in pieces". ""
– Richard Kadrey

Color Me into Your Dream:
"Loneliness is what you feel when the streetlamps outshine
the lamps".

Flowers of Emptiness:
"I said nothing for a time, just ran my fingertips along the edge
of the human-shaped emptiness that had been left inside me."
– Haruki Murakami, Blind Willow, Sleeping Woman

Drink the Wine:
"It is better to love wisely, no doubt: but to love foolishly is
better than not to be able to love at all.""""
— William Makepeace Thackeray

Earthen Fragrance:
Most Memorable Moment(s) in 2017

Nickel Plated:
"Bad Company, I can't deny. Bad Company, Till the Day I
Die". ... by Bad Company

Intoxicating Passion:
When love is not madness-It is not love.

About the Author

The titles of **Edward V. Bonner's** poetry suggests some ways in which the poems inside balance the universe. Most of the poems examine the themes of beauty and risk, pleasure and danger, in the context of one of three kinds of relationships: to romantic partners, to the spiritual world, and to the world of nature. But while these concerns are shared by much of humanity, Bonner's poems sound consistently personal.

As a young child, Ed grew up in a rough area of Pittsburgh Pennsylvania, a small mill town called Hazelwood. Raised by his mother and grandparents until the age of 13. (As Edward Fromen) His mother remarried. At 15 years old he was adopted by his stepfather.

Growing up Bonner got into trouble like most city kids. Only he was the lucky one.

An avid outdoorsman

6 degree black belt in Shotokan karate

Holds an associate degree in business

Holds aeronautics degree and an A&P license.

Author of "*One Kiss- Just One Kiss*"

Author of "*Through the Eyes of a Lost Boy*"

Published in "Adelaide" literary magazine (*Purple Dawn*) Year III Number 11, January 2018.

Published in "Adelaide" literary magazine (*Beyond the Heavens*) Year III Number14, July 2018.

Finalist: ADELAIDE VOICES LITERARY CONTEST 2018 "*Verdant Whisper*".

Edward Bonner grew up in a rough area of Pittsburgh Pennsylvania, a small mill town called Hazelwood. An avid outdoorsman, he holds degrees in business and aeronautics, an A&P license, and 6th degree black belt in Shotokan karate. He is the author of poetry collections One Kiss – Just One Kiss and Through the Eyes of a Lost Boy. A regular contributor to Adelaide Literary Magazine, he is the Finalist of the Adelaide Voices Literary Contest 2018.

9 7 9 8 2 1 8 3 4 5 0 4 4